WINDOW on Britain 2

Video Guide

Richard MacAndrew

OXFORD

UNIVERSITY PRESS

OXFORD
UNIVERSITY PRESS

Great Clarendon Street, Oxford OX2 6DP

Oxford University Press is a department of the University of Oxford.
It furthers the University's objective of excellence in research, scholarship,
and education by publishing worldwide in

Oxford New York

Auckland Cape Town Dar es Salaam Hong Kong Karachi
Kuala Lumpur Madrid Melbourne Mexico City Nairobi
New Delhi Shanghai Taipei Toronto

With offices in

Argentina Austria Brazil Chile Czech Republic France Greece
Guatemala Hungary Italy Japan South Korea Poland Portugal
Singapore Switzerland Thailand Turkey Ukraine Vietnam

OXFORD and OXFORD ENGLISH are registered trade marks of
Oxford University Press in the UK and in certain other countries

© Oxford University Press 2001

The moral rights of the author have been asserted

Database right Oxford University Press (maker)

First published 2001
2011 2010
10 9 8 7

Photocopying

ISBN: 978 0 19 459303 8   Activity Book
ISBN: 978 0 19 459304 5   Video Guide
ISBN: 978 0 19 459300 7   VHS PAL
ISBN: 978 0 19 459301 4   VHS SECAM
ISBN: 978 0 19 459302 1   VHS NTSC

Printed in China

ACKNOWLEDGEMENT

Richard MacAndrew has asserted his right to be identified as the Author of
the Work in accordance with the Copyright, Designs and Patents Act 1988.

Contents

Introduction

Window on Britain 2 is a series of eight units. Like *Window on Britain* each unit examines a different aspect of life in Britain. The accompanying Activity Book provides a variety of exercises for both class use and homework. These exercises help students towards an understanding of each video unit and then develop and extend the particular theme through a variety of speaking activities. A grammar focus is provided in the Language Window. Each unit also has a reading passage and a writing activity which can be used in class or set as homework.

This Video Guide contains an outline of the course, a brief résumé of some basic classroom video techniques, full teaching notes for each unit, answers to the exercises and a transcript.

Teachers can find more information on the subjects in *Window on Britain 2* in *Britain, The country and its People: an introduction for learners of English* by James O'Driscoll, published by Oxford University Press, 1997.

Activity Book outline

Each unit in the Activity Book follows the same basic steps.

Before you watch

This section is designed to allow the teacher to find out what the students already know about a topic. It begins with a Quiz Window where students can test their knowledge. Teachers should stress that students are not expected to be able to answer all (or indeed any) of the questions at the beginning of the lesson but that by the end they should know all the answers.

The Quiz Window also provides a global viewing alternative for each unit. Teachers who want their students to watch a whole unit straight through without pausing can use the Quiz Window as an activity to focus students' attention while they watch. The follow-up viewing can then be divided up into sequences so that students can work through the other exercises.

The Before you watch section also contains a Word Window which introduces some of the new vocabulary students will meet in the unit. Other vocabulary which students might find useful is listed in the teaching notes.

While you watch

This section provides a variety of viewing activities designed to help students understand the video. The activities focus on both linguistic and visual elements of the units.

The Review activity looks back at the Quiz Window and gives students a chance to complete their answers. You may wish to replay the whole unit at this point. This will give students a final opportunity to complete the answers. It will also give them a chance to watch the whole unit from start to finish and realise how much they can now understand.

After you watch

This section contains a variety of exercises concentrating on speaking. Students are required to work in pairs or groups recycling, developing and extending the language and topic of each unit. An explicit focus on grammar is provided in the Language Window with a grammar summary taken from the video and consolidation exercises.

Read and write

This section contains a reading text and writing activity linked by theme to the topic of each unit. These exercises can be done in class or set for homework.

Cultural background

Notes and extra information is given on culturally interesting items.

Language content

This video is primarily topic-based and does not therefore follow a strict structural grading. However, account has been taken of the language level of students at whom the video is aimed and the language that they are likely to be familiar with. There is a light structural grading and particular grammar points are dealt with in the following order:

Unit 1

Review of Present continuous, Present simple, Past simple, and the future with *going to*

Unit 2

Countables and uncountables

Unit 3

Comparatives and superlatives

Unit 4

Future with *will* and *going to*

Unit 5

Present perfect

Unit 6

Present perfect v. Past simple

Unit 7

Open conditionals

Unit 8

Present and Past simple passive

Viewing techniques

Viewing in sequences

At this level students will probably find the units easier to understand if the viewing is broken up into short sequences as indicated in the Activity Book. However, for variety and / or with a strong class teachers may want classes from time to time to view a whole unit straight through. In that case the Quiz Window can be used as a global viewing activity.

No sound

Students can view a sequence of the unit without sound. This can be used to focus students' attention on the pictures and thus becomes an observation activity. Alternatively, it can be used to focus on what the soundtrack might be and students can try and reconstruct or predict the language that is missing.

No vision

Students listen to the sound without the pictures. If your video recorder does not have a facility for playing the sound without the pictures, a coat or blanket thrown over the screen is a very effective way of achieving the same effect (or 'blu-tak' a piece of card to the screen). Students concentrate on the sounds and / or language they hear and then discuss what the pictures might be.

Freeze frame

The teacher pauses the video at a particular moment. This technique can be used to discuss the picture at the point the video is paused. This may be to talk about the content of the video or even just to look at particular vocabulary items in the picture. The technique can also be used to discuss what has just happened or what is going to happen next.

Opening sequence

Some teachers may work through *Window on Britain 2* on a unit-by-unit basis, starting with Unit 1 and going through to the end. Others may prefer to dip into the material using units as they wish so that the material fits in with the other course material that they are using. Both approaches are, of course, equally valid.

Teachers who start *Window on Britain 2* by using Unit 1 (whether they continue with Unit 2 or a completely different unit) will have the option of exploiting the opening introductory sequence in class.

1 Work

Topic content

This unit looks at different aspects of work in Britain: facts and figures about the working population, important industries, how work has changed over the last hundred years. We also meet some British people and find out how they feel about their jobs.

Teachers can find out more information on this subject in *Britain, The Country and its People: an introduction for learners of English* by James O'Driscoll, published by Oxford University Press, 1997.

Language focus

Review of Present continuous, Present simple, Past simple, future with *going to*

Vocabulary content

population, unemployed, full-time, part-time, to retire, industry, industrial, to manufacture, shipyard, to develop, to produce, financial, to retail, hi-tech, convenient

---

Suggested procedures

◆ Use the Quiz Window to arouse students' interest and find out how much they already know about the topic area. Do not go through the answers until after the students have viewed the unit.

◆ Use the Word Window to familiarize students with some of the new vocabulary they are likely to meet. Introduce other suggested vocabulary if necessary.

◆ Work through the video and the activities sequence by sequence. You may need to play the sequences more than once so that students gain a satisfactory understanding. Use the Review activity for a final global viewing.

◆ Alternatively, you may want to play the whole unit through once straightaway. You can use the Quiz Window to focus students' attention while doing this. The follow-up viewing can then be divided into sections so that students can work through the other activities.

◆ The Language Window draws a particular grammar point from the unit, highlights it, and provides follow-up exercises and reinforcement.

◆ The **After you watch** and **Read and write** sections provide a variety of topic-linked follow-up activities.

Opening sequence ☐☐☐☐

(up to: ... *environment, health, and law and order.*)

◆ Ask students to look at the activity on the Introduction page of the Activity Book. Explain what *Window on Britain 2* is about. Give students time to do the exercise.

▶ Play the sequence.

◆ Accept any answers that students can justify. Students will not find out if they are right or wrong until they have viewed the whole video and that will not be happening in this lesson! The point of the activity is to raise awareness of the content of *Window on Britain 2* so that students will know what to expect when they use it in future lessons.

Before you watch

These **Before you watch** activities are designed to arouse students' interest in the topic and pre-teach some of the vocabulary necessary for understanding the unit.

Quiz Window

◆ Find out what students already know about work in Britain: numbers of people who work and are unemployed, important industries, and how work has changed over the last 100 years.

◆ Put students in pairs to complete the Quiz Window. Stress that they are not expected to be able to answer all the questions in the Quiz Window, but that by the end of the lesson they should have all the answers. Encourage students to speculate on the answers as this will motivate them to watch the unit.

◆ The answers to the Quiz Window are given in the Review section.

Word Window

◆ Ask the students to circle the correct words in the sentences. They should use dictionaries if necessary.

Key:

1 a company; b full-time; c permanent;
d manufacturer; e produced; f unemployed

◆ Students should then complete this exercise with the words that they did not circle in exercise 1.

Key:

2 a temporary; b retired; c developed; d factory;
e part-time; f builder

While you watch

To help students' comprehension of the programme, the viewing is split up into five sequences.

Sequence 1 ☐☐☐☐

(up to: ... *people work in the building industry.*)

1 Ask students to look at the different pictures and check that they understand what's happening in each picture. They do not necessarily need to be able to explain it in English.

🎞 Play the sequence so that students can tick the activities they see.

Key:

1 ✓; 2 ✗; 3 ✓; 4 ✓; 5 ✗

2 Ask students to read through the sentences and complete as many sentences as they can before viewing the sequence again.

🎞 Play the sequence again for students to complete the sentences and make any necessary changes.

Key:

a – 59; b – 15; c – 12; d – 16; e – 1.5; f – 44, 65;
g – 31, 60; h – 1

Sequence 2 ☐☐☐☐

(up to: ... *they produce about 200 cars a day.*)

◆ Ask students to look at the notes and think about the words that might be missing.

🎞 Play the sequence. If necessary, play it twice so that students have time to write down all the information.

Key:

1 manufacturing; 2 factories; 3 Wales; 4 north; 5 cotton;
6 ships; 7 1935; 8 1951; 9 1989; 10 over 2,000;
11 about 200

Sequence 3 ☐☐☐☐

(up to: ... *they were days when banks closed.*)

◆ Put students in pairs to read through the sentences and decide if they think they will be true or false.

🎞 Play the sequence while students mark the sentences. Give students time to correct the false sentences. Play the sequence again, if necessary.

Key:

a T; b F – It's first in Europe, number three in the world;
c T; d T; e – only four; f T; g F – only 20 days;
h F – only eight public holidays

Sequence 4 ☐☐☐☐

(up to: *Rain!*)

There is a lot of information in this sequence – far too much for one student to assimilate on his or her own. In the first exercise students are asked to find out the job of each person in the sequence. In the second activity students should find out information about one person only.

1 Ask students to look at the pictures and predict what jobs they think the people might do.

🎞 Play the sequence. Give students time to compare their answers.

Key:

1 (schoolteacher); 2 helicopter pilot; 3 bookseller;
4 sales rep; 5 lecturer; 6 airline pilot; 7 Oxford Walking Tour Guide

2 Explain that students only need to find out information about one of the people. Put the students into groups and check that each person in the group knows who they are finding out about. Make sure each member of the group has chosen a different person on the video!

   ▶ Play the sequence (twice if necessary).

Now students should compare the answers and complete the information about the other five people.

Key:

1 (schoolteacher)
   (about 60 during term time)
   (long holidays)
   (working at weekends)

2 helicopter pilot
   30–40
   getting home every night
   getting up at 5 in the morning

3 bookseller
   37 and a half
   serving customers
   –

4 sales rep
   60–80
   freedom
   –

5 lecturer
   12 contact hours
   meeting young people
   administration / paper work

6 pilot
   20 flying; 50 working
   it's fun
   folding shirts before a trip

7 Oxford Walking Tour Guide
   3–7 days a week
   meeting people from all round the world
   rain

Sequence 5 ☐☐☐☐

(to the end)

◆ Give students a little time to look at the questions.

   ▶ Play the sequence while students answer the questions.

Key:

a Because more and more people are on-line.
b Well over half a million.
c It's easy, convenient, and you can have a cup of tea when you want one.

Review

Students should go back and add to or change what they have written in the Quiz Window. You may like to play the sequence again all the way through.

Quiz Window Key:

1 27 million;
2 1 finance, 2 technology, 3 retailing, 4 manufacturing, 5 shipbuilding; shipbuilding & manufacturing were important in 19th century; retailing, finance & technology are important now;
3 bank holidays;
4 it depends where you live!

After you watch

Game

Explain the game to the students. Play it once with the whole class so that everyone understands what to do. Put students in groups to play the game. Go round the class helping where necessary and noting any mistakes that may need to be dealt with later.

Discussion

Explain the task to the students. Put them in groups to agree on an order of importance.

Have a class feedback session so that students can find out what the other groups thought.

Language Window

◆ Give students time to complete the tense review box.

Key:

TENSE	USE	EXAMPLE(S)
Present simple	• to talk about things that are generally true	• *Most people work full-time.* • *How many hours do they work?*
Present continuous	• to talk about things happening now	• *We're now living in the twenty-first century.*
Past simple	• to talk about events that happened in finished past time	• *Other industries developed in the twentieth century.* • *Ford bought Jaguar in 1989.*
Future with *going to*	• to talk about people's intentions	• *We're going to look at some important areas of British life.* • *We're also going to look at the environment.*

◆ Sort out any problems that arise from the tense review box. Then ask students to complete the exercise.

Key:

a 's raining; b 're going to be; c worked; d 'm trying; e are / going to do; f does not / arrive; g Did / meet; h Do / know

Read and write

These activities can be done in class or for homework. You may wish to pre-teach these words before students look at the reading passage: *service, comments, to serve, vital, low-cost airline, delicious, salmon.*

1 This activity encourages students to read for the general meaning of each paragraph.

Key:

What happens in a typical day?
How important is your job?
Is there anything you dislike about your job?
Do things sometimes go wrong?
What question do people always ask you about your job?

2 This activity requires students to read the text again for more detailed meaning.

Key:

a F; b F; c F; d T; e T; f F

3 Students should write their own 'WHAT I DO?' article. In class give students time to decide who they might interview about their job – if it can be an English speaker so much the better! They should then conduct the interview outside class time. The article can be written up in class or for homework.

2 Holidays

Topic content

This unit looks at different aspects of what the British do on holiday: where they go, what they do, where they stay, and how long they have.

Teachers can find out more information on this subject in *Britain, The Country and its People: an introduction for learners of English* by James O'Driscoll, published by Oxford University Press, 1997.

Language focus

Countables and uncountables

Vocabulary content

a break, a holidaymaker, traditional, to windsurf, a deckchair, a narrowboat, relaxing

Suggested procedures

◆ Use the Quiz Window to arouse students' interest and find out how much they already know about the topic area. Do not go through the answers until after the students have viewed the unit.

◆ Use the Word Window to familiarize students with some of the new vocabulary they are likely to meet. Introduce other suggested vocabulary if necessary.

◆ Work through the video and the activities sequence by sequence. You may need to play the sequences more than once so that students gain a satisfactory understanding. Use the Review activity for a final global viewing.

◆ Alternatively, you may want to play the whole unit through once straightaway. You can use the Quiz Window to focus students' attention while doing this. The follow-up viewing can then be divided into sections so that students can work through the other activities.

◆ The Language Window draws a particular grammar point from the unit, highlights it, and provides follow-up exercises and reinforcement.

◆ The **After you watch** and **Read and write** sections provide a variety of topic-linked follow-up activities.

Before you watch

These **Before you watch** activities are designed to arouse students' interest in the topic and pre-teach some of the vocabulary necessary for understanding the unit.

Quiz Window

◆ Find out what students already know about what the British do on holiday: where they go, what they do, where they stay, and how long they have.

◆ Put students in pairs to complete the Quiz Window. Stress that they are not expected to be able to answer all the questions in the Quiz Window but that by the end of the lesson they should have all the answers. Encourage students to speculate on the answers as this will motivate them to watch the unit.

◆ The answers to the Quiz Window are given in the Review section.

Word Window

◆ Ask students to put the words in the correct places. They should use dictionaries if necessary.

Key:

AT THE AIRPORT	THINGS TO DO
• customs	• swim
• destination	• windsurf
• departure lounge	• sunbathe
• passport	• climb

PLACES TO STAY	THINGS AT THE SEASIDE
• hotel	• deckchair
• guest house	• ice-cream
• campsite	• towel
• bed & breakfast	• pier

While you watch

To help students' comprehension of the unit, the viewing is split up into three sequences.

Sequence 1 ▢▢▢▢

(up to: *Sometimes there isn't very much sun.*)

1 Let students look at the list of places so that they know what they are listening for.

   ▶ Play the sequence while students tick the places they hear.

   Key:

   Florida ✓   the USA ✗

   the Caribbean ✓   Brazil ✗

   Western Europe ✓   Spain ✓

   Greece ✗   France ✗

2 Students should look at the sentences and decide if they are true or false.

   ▶ Play the sequence again and give students time to check and / or change their answers.

   Key:

   a F; b F: c T; d T; e T

Sequence 2 ▢▢▢▢

(up to: *Everyone hopes for a lot of sunshine and not too much rain!*)

1 Allow students to look at the pictures and check that they know what they are looking for.

   ▶ Play the sequence while students tick the appropriate pictures.

   Key:

   1; 2; 4; 5

2 Check that students understand what information they are trying to find.

   ▶ Play the sequence. Give students time to compare their answers if necessary.

   Key:

   a a lot of sunshine / not too much rain
   b cars, planes
   c Blackpool, Bournemouth, Brighton
   d swim, windsurf, sunbathe, sit in a deckchair
   e hotel, guest house, bed & breakfast, tent, caravan

Sequence 3 ▢▢▢▢

(to the end)

1 See if students can complete the map before they watch the sequence.

   ▶ Play the sequence.

   Key:

   a Scotland; b The Lake District; c London; d (Devon);
   e Cornwall

2 Students can try this exercise before watching the sequence again.

   ▶ Play the sequence while students check and / or change their answers.

   Key:

   yachting ✗   hang-gliding ✗

   climbing ✓   walking ✓

   cycling ✓   sailing on a narrowboat ✓

3 Give students time to discuss this question. If students are interested, have a class round-up to see what everyone thinks.

Review

Students should go back and add to or change what they have written in the Quiz Window. You may like to play the sequence again all the way through.

Quiz Window Key:

1 b July and August; 2 c Spain; 3 a 100 kilometres;
4 b there are lots of things to do; 5 c 250,000

After you watch

Problem solving

Explain the task to the students. Explain also that there is no right answer to this activity. Put the students in groups to discuss the problem and come up with some solutions. Go round the class noting mistakes to be dealt with later and helping out with language where necessary.

Have a class round-up session where different groups put forward their solutions.

Discussion

Explain the different parts of the discussion. Put students in groups to work through the different tasks. Go round the class noting mistakes to be dealt with later and helping out with language where necessary. Then put groups together to compare their answers. Alternatively, have a class round-up and find out what each group decided.

Language Window

◆ Go through the language summary with the class.

◆ Ask the students to do the exercises either individually or in pairs.

Key:

1 a any, some; b any; c any; d some; e Some

2 a many; b a lot of; c many; d much; e much; f a lot of

3 a *few* tourists; b a *little* fish; c so *little* rain; d a *little* cake; e correct; f a *little* money

Read and write

These activities can be done in class or for homework.

1 Students should read through the postcard quickly and identify where the different phrases go.

  1 And it's beautiful

  2 Then we hired a car

  3 The only problem is the weather

  4 Then we're going to drive down to Glasgow

2 Students should read the postcard again more slowly and answer the questions.

  a In Scotland – on the island of Harris.

  b Windy, not very warm, and it rains a lot.

  c They are walking a lot (and sitting by the log fire in the evenings).

  d A few more days.

  e Glasgow.

3 Students can write their postcards in class or for homework.

3 Animals

Topic content

This unit looks at animals in Britain: farm animals, wild animals, pets, working animals and animals used for sport. It also looks at British attitudes to animals and what happens when animals get sick.

Language focus

Comparatives and superlatives

Vocabulary content

in the wild, turkey, deer, badger, hedgehog, spines, fox, habit, protection, squirrel, eagle, protected species, common, rare, to control, to protect, tortoise, goldfish

Suggested procedures

◆ Use the Quiz Window to arouse students' interest and find out how much they already know about the topic area. Do not go through the answers until after the students have viewed the unit.

◆ Use the Word Window to familiarize students with some of the new vocabulary they are likely to meet. Introduce other suggested vocabulary if necessary.

◆ Work through the video and the activities sequence by sequence. You may need to play the sequences more than once so that students gain a satisfactory understanding. Use the Review activity for a final global viewing.

◆ Alternatively, you may want to play the whole unit through once straightaway. You can use the Quiz Window to focus students' attention while doing this. The follow-up viewing can then be divided into sections so that students can work through the other activities.

◆ The Language Window draws a particular grammar point from the unit, highlights it, and provides follow-up exercises and reinforcement.

◆ The After you watch and Read and write sections provide a variety of topic-linked follow-up activities.

Before you watch

These **Before you watch** activities are designed to arouse students' interest in the topic and pre-teach some of the vocabulary necessary for understanding the unit.

Quiz Window

◆ Find out what students already know about British animals: what types of animals you can find in Britain, what the British like to keep as pets, and British attitudes towards pets.

◆ Put students in pairs to complete the Quiz Window. Stress that they are not expected to be able to answer all the questions in the Quiz Window but that by the end of the lesson they should have all the answers. Encourage students to speculate on the answers as this will motivate them to watch the unit.

◆ The answers to the Quiz Window are given in the Review section.

Word Window

◆ Ask students to match the words to the pictures. They should use dictionaries if necessary.

Key:
1 chicken
2 pig
3 duck
4 deer
5 sheep
6 turkey
7 hedgehog
8 squirrel
9 swan
10 badger
11 cow
12 fox
13 mouse
14 eagle
15 rabbit

While you watch

To help students' comprehension of the unit, the viewing is split up into five sequences.

Sequence 1 ☐☐☐☐

(**up to:** ... *an amazing 172 million farm birds.*)

◆ Check that students understand both exercise 1 and 2.

    Play the sequence while students tick the appropriate animals.

    Play the sequence again while students complete the right-hand column.

Key:

✓	ANIMALS	NUMBER IN BRITAIN
✓	cows	11 million
✓	pigs	7 million
✓	sheep	44.5 million
	turkeys	
	ducks	172 million
✓	chickens	

Sequence 2 ☐☐☐☐

(**up to:** ... *116 protected species of animal in Britain.*)

1 Explain that students will see quite a long sequence about British wild animals, and that all they have to do on the first viewing is number the animals in the order they appear.

    Play the sequence while students number the pictures.

Key:

1 fallow deer, 2 field mouse, 3 red deer, 4 badger, 5 rabbit, 6 hedgehog, 7 fox, 8 red squirrel, 9 grey squirrel, 10 golden eagle

2 Students should now watch the sequence again and complete the notes about each animal. You may wish to pause the video for a few seconds after each animal so that students have time to write their answers.

    Play the sequence again.

Key:

fallow deer:	all over
field mouse:	smallest
red deer:	largest, Scottish
badger:	nose, night
rabbit:	early, evening
hedgehog:	spines
fox:	country, towns
red squirrel:	200, Scotland, parts
grey squirrel:	North America, (a little bit) bigger, finding food
golden eagle:	800, protected

Sequence 3 ☐☐☐☐

(**up to:** *It's amazing, isn't it?*)

◆ You may like students to try and match the sentence halves before they view the sequence. Alternatively, just give them time to read the halves so that they are prepared for the sequence.

    Play the sequence.

Key:

1 People use horses for sports such as racing and polo. The police use horses to control crowds.
2 The RSPCA (Royal Society for Prevention of Cruelty to Animals) started in 1824. The RSPB (Royal Society for the Protection of Birds) started in 1889.
3 In Britain there are 8 million cats, 7 million dogs and 28 million fish.

Sequence 4 ☐☐☐☐

(**up to:** *He's a rabbit.*)

◆ Check that students understand both activities

    Play the sequence twice so that students have time to complete both exercises.

Key:

	PET	NAME
1	(a dog)	(Henry)
2	a cat	Katy
3	a kitten	Rasputin
4	a tortoise	Harry
5	a goldfish	Oxo
6	a rabbit	Barney

Sequence 5 ☐☐☐☐

(to the end)

◆ Explain to the class that they may find this sequence difficult. However, they should be able to understand enough of what is going on to be able to answer the questions. They do not need to understand every word. Give them time to look at the questions.

   ▶ Play the sequence. Then give students time to talk to each other and compare their answers. If necessary, play the sequence again.

Key:

a take it to the vet; b it disappeared and came back with an injured leg; c five full-time and two part-time; d dogs, cats and rabbits

Review

Students should go back and add to or change what they have written in the Quiz Window. You may like to play the sequence again all the way through.

Quiz Window Key:

a ✗; b ✓; c ✓; d ✗; e ✓; f ✗; g ✓; h ✓

After you watch

Survey

◆ Go through the instructions with the class and check that they understand what to do. Put the students into groups of 5 or 6 to exchange information.

◆ Have a class feedback session to pool information and build up a pet profile of the class. Either display the information on the board or put it on a poster, which you can leave on the classroom wall.

Discussion

◆ Go through the instructions for the discussion, checking that students know what to do. If necessary, discuss the advantages and disadvantages of one of the animals with the whole class before putting students into groups. Make sure students are aware there are not necessarily any right answers.

Students should then discuss the different animals in groups.

Language Window

◆ Go through the language summary with the class.

◆ Ask students to do the exercises either individually or in pairs.

Key:

1 answer to the example: the blue whale
   1 What's the tallest animal in the world? – the giraffe
   2 What's the fastest animal on land? – the cheetah
   3 What's the most dangerous land snake in the world? – the fierce snake from Australia
   4 Where can you find the most poisonous frog in the world? – western Colombia – the golden poison arrow frog
   5 Where can you find the most dangerous jellyfish in the world? – Australia – box jellyfish
   6 Where can you find the longest crocodile in the world? – Bhitarkanika Wildlife Sanctuary, Orissa, India – over 7m long

2 a cheaper, b more dangerous, c smaller, d bigger, e more comfortable, f worse

Read and write

These activities can be done in class or for homework.

1 This activity encourages students to read for gist. Students may need some vocabulary preparation for this article: rooftop, security check, equipment, cage, tunnel, sniffing, frightened.

   Alternatively, you may prefer to let them use their dictionaries when they need to. Stress that it is not necessary to understand every word.

   Key:

   Fox gets RSPCA royal treatment is the best answer. The other two headlines are not correct.

2 Students should read the text again more carefully and choose the correct answers.

   Key:

   1 b; 2 a; 3 c

3 Students should write their own newspaper article based on the picture story. If students have an animal story of their own, you may prefer to let them write about that.

4 Media

Topic content

This unit looks at different aspects of the British media: newspapers and magazines, television, radio and the Internet.

Teachers can find out more information on this subject in *Britain, The Country and its People: an introduction for learners of English* by James O'Driscoll, published by Oxford University Press, 1997.

> ## Language focus
>
> Future with *will* and *going to*
>
> ## Vocabulary content
>
> the media, tabloid, broadsheet, quality, online, website, terrestrial, commercial, advertising, a television licence, satellite, cable

Suggested procedures

◆ Use the Quiz Window to arouse students' interest and find out how much they already know about the topic area. Do not go through the answers until after the students have viewed the unit.

◆ Use the Word Window to familiarize students with some of the new vocabulary they are likely to meet. Introduce other suggested vocabulary if necessary.

◆ Work through the video and the activities sequence by sequence. You may need to play the sequences more than once so that students gain a satisfactory understanding. Use the Review activity for a final global viewing.

◆ Alternatively, you may want to play the whole unit through once straightaway. You can use the Quiz Window to focus students' attention while doing this. The follow-up viewing can then be divided into sections so that students can work through the other activities.

◆ The Language Window draws a particular grammar point from the unit, highlights it, and provides follow-up exercises and reinforcement.

◆ The **After you watch** and **Read and write** sections provide a variety of topic-linked follow-up activities.

Before you watch

These **Before you watch** activities are designed to arouse students' interest in the topic and pre-teach some of the vocabulary necessary for understanding the unit.

Quiz Window

◆ Find out what students already know about the British media. Do they know any British newspapers or magazines? Do they know any British television or radio stations? Do they visit any British websites?

◆ Put students in pairs to complete the Quiz Window. Stress that they are not expected to be able to answer all the questions in the Quiz Window but that by the end of the lesson they should have all the answers. Encourage students to speculate on the answers as this will motivate them to watch the unit.

◆ The answers to the Quiz Window are given in the Review section.

Word Window

◆ Point out to students that this is a collocation exercise. For example, a 'quality newspaper' is a common collocation in English. However, we do not usually talk about 'quality television channels', even though some are obviously better than others.

Key:

	national	satellite	quality	cable	popular	terrestrial	local	broadsheet	tabloid	commercial
newspapers	✓		✓		✓		✓	✓	✓	
TV stations	✓	✓		✓	✓	✓			✓	
radio stations	✓				✓		✓		✓	

While you watch

To help students' comprehension of the unit, the viewing is split up into five sequences.

Sequence 1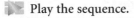

(up to: ... *who use the Internet is increasing all the time.*)

1 Check that students understand what to do.

   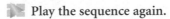 Play the sequence.

   Key:

   The Sun; The Daily Mirror; The Times;
   The Daily Telegraph; The Independent;
   The Daily Express; The Oxford Times; London Wedding;
   Vogue

2 Give students time to read through the notes. In a strong class they may already be able to fill in some of the answers having only watched the sequence once.

   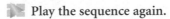 Play the sequence. If necessary pause the video at appropriate points so that students are able to complete the notes.

   Key:

   1 Sun; 2 2.25; 3 human interest; 4 serious;

   5 quality; 6 Daily Telegraph; 7 700,000; 8 The Guardian; 9 articles; 10 pictures;

   11 130; 12 6,500

Sequence 2 ▢▢▢▢

(up to: ... *have a television in their bedroom.*)

1 Explain the task to the students. See the introduction for how to deal with this activity if your video player does not have a 'sound only' facility. Allow the students a few minutes to discuss their ideas on what the pictures might be. Elicit answers from different groups so that there is a pool of ideas before students start watching.

   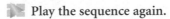 Play the sequence.

2 Give students time either as a class or in their groups to discuss the differences between their ideas and what they actually saw.

3 Students should make 11 sentences from the box.

4 Students should answer the questions.

   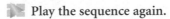 Play the sequence again if necessary.

Key:

3 The BBC has 5 national radio stations.
   The BBC has 39 local radio stations.
   The BBC has two terrestrial television channels.
   The BBC is not commercial.
   The BBC uses money from TV licences to pay for programmes.
   ITV is a commercial TV channel.
   Channel 4 is a commercial TV channel.
   Channel 5 is a commercial TV channel.
   ITV has advertising during its programmmes.
   Channel 4 has advertising during its programmmes.
   Channel 5 has advertising during its programmmes.

4 a Lots; b 46%

Sequence 3 ▢▢▢▢

(up to: *I'll probably watch Top Of The Pops and Friends.*)

1 You could introduce this sequence by finding out how many students in the class like *The Simpsons*, and, if there is a programme like *Top Of The Pops* in your country, how many students like that.

Cultural background

Top Of The Pops is a weekly BBC programme which looks at the pop charts. It shows current pop videos and bands play live in the studio.

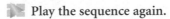 Play the sequence.

Key:
a three; b two

2 This time students have to listen for more detail.

   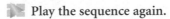 Play the sequence again.

Key:

a five / all of them; b one; c one; d four (Trick question! It's not five – one person says it twice!)

Sequence 4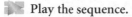

(up to: ... *comedy videos.*)

◆ As an introduction to this sequence, discuss what sort of videos the class like to watch. Give students a few moments to look at the speech bubbles.

   ▮▮ Play the sequence.

Key:

1 action, science fiction; 2 comedy ; 3 old films; 4 skateboarding, rollerblading; 5 comedy

Sequence 5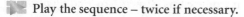

(to the end)

◆ Give students a moment or two to look at the sentences.

   ▮▮ Play the sequence – twice if necessary.

Key:

a F; b F

Review

Students should go back and add to or change what they have written in the Quiz Window. You may like to play the sequence again all the way through.

Quiz Window Key:

1 About 26 million; 2 many of the important British newspapers are mentioned in the video; 3 see answers in Sequence 1; 4 online; 5 BBC, ITV, Channel 4, Channel 5; 6 almost 24 hours a week; 7 84%

After you watch

Class survey

◆ Students should work in groups of three or four, going through the survey and making a note of their answers.

◆ Have a class feedback session and collate the results. Display them on the board or, better still, on a poster which can become a wall display in the classroom.

Problem solving

◆ Make sure that students understand the situation. Then put them in groups to plan their evening.

◆ Have a class feedback session so that students can find out what the other groups are doing. If you like, the class could vote on which group is going to have the best evening.

Language Window

◆ Go through the language summary with the class.

◆ Students should do the exercises individually or in pairs.

Key:

1 1 Turn the TV on. It'll be time for the news.
   2 Don't worry! The bus'll be here in a few minutes.
   3 It's really hot in here. I'll open the window.
   4 I'm so tired. I think I'll go to bed early tonight.
   5 I'm going on holiday. I won't be back until next week.
   6 I think I'll buy some new shoes. These ones have got holes in.

2 (example answers)
   a She's going for a drive.
   b He's going to have some toast.
   c They're going to play tennis.
   d She's going to sit in the sun.
   e He's going to watch TV.

3 a 'll
   b 's going to
   c 'll
   d 'm going to
   e 'll

Read and write

These activities can be done in class or for homework.

1 Students should read through the information quickly to decide which film they would like to see.

2 They will need to read the reviews more carefully for this question.

Key:

a Chocolat; b Crouching Tiger Hidden Dragon; c Traffic

3 Students can write this in class or for homework.

5 Leisure

Topic content

This unit looks at different aspects of how the British spend their leisure time both at home and outside the home.

Teachers can find out more information on this subject in *Britain, The Country and its People: an introduction for learners of English* by James O'Driscoll, published by Oxfors University Press, 1997.

Language focus

Present perfect

Vocabulary content

to skateboard, to rollerblade, rock climbing, a karaoke competition, historic, a sculpture, a collection, an attraction

Suggested procedures

◆ Use the Quiz Window to arouse students' interest and find out how much they already know about the topic area. Do not go through the answers until after the students have viewed the unit.

◆ Use the Word Window to familiarize students with some of the new vocabulary they are likely to meet. Introduce other suggested vocabulary if necessary.

◆ Work through the video and the activities sequence by sequence. You may need to play the sequences more than once so that students gain a satisfactory understanding. Use the Review activity for a final global viewing.

◆ Alternatively, you may want to play the whole unit through once straightaway. You can use the Quiz Window to focus students' attention while doing this. The follow-up viewing can then be divided into sections so that students can work through the other activities.

◆ The Language Window draws a particular grammar point from the unit, highlights it, and provides follow-up exercises and reinforcement.

◆ The After you watch and Read and write sections provide a variety of topic-linked follow-up activities.

Before you watch

These **Before you watch** activities are designed to arouse students' interest in the topic and pre-teach some of the vocabulary necessary for understanding the unit.

Quiz Window

◆ Find out what students already know about how the British spend their leisure time. Do they think it will be similar to the way they, the students, spend their leisure time or will it be very different?

◆ Put students in pairs to complete the Quiz Window. Stress that they are not expected to be able to answer all the questions in the Quiz Window but that by the end of the lesson they should have all the answers. Encourage students to speculate on the answers as this will motivate them to watch the unit.

◆ The answers to the Quiz Window are given in the Review section.

Word Window

◆ Ask students to match the words to the activities.

Key:
1 sailing
2 parachuting
3 surfing
4 skateboarding
5 rally driving
6 rock climbing
7 canoeing
8 horseracing
9 rollerblading
10 snowboarding

◆ Put students in pairs to find out if their partner has done any of the activities. You could wait till after you have played Sequence 1 before finding out which activities members of the class have done.

While you watch

To help students' comprehension of the unit, the viewing is split up into six sequences.

Sequence 1 ☐☐☐☐

(up to: *Have you tried any of these?*)

◆ This is a visual activity. Ask students to tick the activities they see.

▶ Play the sequence.

Key:

The following should be ticked: sailing; surfing; parachuting; rally driving; canoeing; snowboarding

Sequence 2 ☐☐☐☐

(up to: … *a drama group and a dance group.*)

◆ Check that students understand the instructions for both exercises 1 and 2.

▶ Play the sequence while students do exercise 1.

Key:

a two boys; b one girl

▶ Play the sequence again while students do exercise 2.

Key:

The following should be crossed out:
1 (play football)
2 play rugby
3 listen to music
4 skateboard
5 correct
6 play rugby
7 go windsurfing
8 listen to music
9 go to the cinema

Sequence 3 ☐☐☐☐

(up to: … *the number of cinemas has more than doubled too.*)

1 Make sure students understand that they should tick the places where they see Leonie, not the places she mentions.

▶ Play the sequence.

Key:

in a pub; in a fast food restaurant; outside a cinema

2 Give students time to read through the sentences and put in some answers.

▶ Play the sequence again so that students can complete the exercise and change answers if necessary.

Key:

a T; b F; c T; d F; e F; f T

Sequence 4 ☐☐☐☐

(up to: … *admission is free.*)

1 Make sure students understand what to do.

▶ Play the sequence.

Key:

4 watching sport
3 going to discos and nightclubs
1 visiting historic buildings
5 visiting art galleries and museums
2 having a short break holiday

2 Give students time to look at exercises 2 and 3 and work out the answers. Play the sequence again for students to check and / or change their answers.

Key:

2 Kingston Lacy has lovely gardens.
Corfe Castle is over 1000 years old.
The Ashmolean Museum is part of the University of Oxford.

3 a 200,000; b nothing – it is free

Sequence 5 ☐☐☐☐

(up to: … *it's already a very popular tourist attraction.*)

1 Students should tick the places they see.

▶ Play the sequence.

Key:

1 ✓; 2 ✓; 3 ✓; 4 ✓; 5 ✓; 6 ✗

2 Give students time to write in the names.

▶ Play the sequence again so that students can check and/or change their answers.

Key:

1 Tower of London
2 Alton Towers
3 Legoland
4 Madame Tussaud's
5 London Eye

Sequence 6 ▢▢▢▢

(to the end)

◆ Check that students know what to do – there are two parts to the question.

Play the sequence.

Key:

2 reading
1 listening to the radio or CDs
4 watching TV
3 visiting or entertaining friends and family

Watching TV is the most popular activity.

Review

Students should go back and add to or change what they have written in the Quiz Window. You may like to play the sequence again all the way through.

Quiz Window Key:

1 4 going to the library, 2 going to a restaurant, 5 going to the cinema, 3 going to a fast food restaurant, 1 going to the pub

2 visiting historic buildings, short break holidays, going to discos and nightclubs, watching sport, going to museums and art galleries

3 theme parks, museums, historic buildings, the London Eye

4 reading, listening to the radio or CDs, watching TV, visiting or entertaining friends and family

After you watch

Class survey

Make sure students understand what information they are trying to find out. Put them in groups of five or six to exchange information.

Have a class feedback session to answer the two questions.

Pairwork

Make sure students understand the situation. Put students in pairs and allow them time to draw up a plan of action. Then put pairs together so that they can compare ideas. Alternatively, you could have a feedback session where different pairs present their plans to the class.

Language Window

◆ Go through the language summary with the class.

◆ Ask students to do the activities individually or in pairs.

Key:

1 1 Could I speak to Jack, please? I'm afraid he's gone out.
   2 You look well. I've just been on holiday.
   3 Alice is in hospital. She's broken her leg.
   4 Congratulations! You've passed your exam.
   5 I can't find my keys anywhere. Have you seen them?
   6 Do you know Alan's phone number? I've lost my address book.
   7 Where's Anna these days? I haven't seen her for ages.
   8 I've just made some tea. Would you like a cup?

2 free answers

Read and write

These activities can be done in class or for homework.

1 Students should read through the information quickly to decide which place appeals to them most.

2 Students should then read more carefully to find answers to the questions.

Key:

a Lee Valley Park; b Blackpool Tower; c The London Planetarium; d Beaulieu Motor Museum; e Old Trafford; f Chester Zoo in summer

3 Students should choose two or three attractions in their area to write about.

6 Environment

Topic content

This unit looks at different aspects of the environment in Britain: the country side and national parks, towns and cities, the causes and effects of pollution, and what is being done to combat pollution.

Teachers can find out more information on this subject in *Britain, The Country and its People: an introduction for learners of English* by James O'Driscoll, published by Oxford University Press, 1997.

Language focus

Present perfect v. Past simple

Vocabulary content

the environment, national parks, pollution, coal, a threat, traffic-free, crowded, essential, to protect, loads of

Suggested procedures

◆ Use the Quiz Window to arouse students' interest and find out how much they already know about the topic area. Do not go through the answers until after the students have viewed the unit.

◆ Use the Word Window to familiarize students with some of the new vocabulary they are likely to meet. Introduce other suggested vocabulary if necessary.

◆ Work through the video and the activities sequence by sequence. You may need to play the sequences more than once so that students gain a satisfactory understanding. Use the Review activity for a final global viewing.

◆ Alternatively, you may want to play the whole unit through once straightaway. You can use the Quiz Window to focus students' attention while doing this. The follow-up viewing can then be divided into sections so that students can work through the other activities.

◆ The Language Window draws a particular grammar point from the unit, highlights it, and provides follow-up exercises and reinforcement.

◆ The **After you watch** and **Read and write** sections provide a variety of topic-linked follow-up activities.

Before you watch

These **Before you watch** activities are designed to arouse students' interest in the topic and pre-teach some of the vocabulary necessary for understanding the unit.

Quiz Window

◆ Find out what students already know about the environment and environmental problems in Britain. Do they think the environment is very different from that in their own country? How has the British environment changed over the last 100 years? What environmental problems are the British now facing? What measures have the British taken / are the British taking to deal with these problems?

◆ Put students in pairs to complete the Quiz Window. Stress that they are not expected to be able to answer all the questions in the Quiz Window but that by the end of the lesson they should have all the answers. Encourage students to speculate on the answers as this will motivate them to watch the unit.

◆ The answers to the Quiz Window are given in the Review section.

Word Window

◆ Students should work on the exercises individually or in pairs. Allow them to use dictionaries if necessary.

Key:

1 a to create national parks; b to protect the environment; c to take action; d to deal with increasing traffic; e to control pollution; f to burn coal; g to introduce laws

Other collocations are possible, e.g. to create laws / pollution, to introduce national parks, etc.

2 a burn coal; b introduce laws; c created national parks; d take action, control pollution; e protect the environment; f deal with increasing traffic

While you watch

To help students' comprehension of this unit, the viewing is split up into three sequences.

Sequence 1 ▢▢▢▢

(up to: *... visitors every year.*)

1 Explain that students have to predict the type of information that they would expect to hear on the soundtrack and the sort of questions that they would expect to find the answers to.

   Play the sequence without the sound.

   Allow students time to discuss their answers.

2 Play the sequence with the sound. Allow students more time to discuss the differences between what they expected and what they heard.

3 Students should try and answer the questions without watching the sequence again. However, if necessary, allow them to see it one more time.

Key:

a About 1,500 sq km.; b 75%; c a third of the population of Britain; d 22 million

Sequence 2 ▢▢▢▢

(up to: *many other British cities now have traffic free areas.*)

1 You could prepare students for this sequence by asking them to list as many causes of pollution as they can think of. Check they understand what they are looking for.

   Play the sequence without the sound.

Key:

factory chimneys, cars, buses, lorries, aeroplanes

2 Give students time to read through the question and the alternatives.

   Play the sequence with the sound. If necessary, play it again so that students are able to answer all the questions.

Key:

1 c; 2 a; 3 b; 4 b; 5 b

Sequence 3 ▢▢▢▢

(to the end)

◆ Give students time to look through the skeleton for the notes.

   Play the sequence. You may need to play it a couple of times so that students are able to catch the information. Alternatively, you could pause after each person speaks to give students time to make their notes.

Key:

1 areas, walks, walks, families; 2 beautiful, walking; 3 rivers; 4 appetite; 5 countryside, wildlife; 6 see, walks, friendly, nice

Review

Students should go back and add to or change what they have written in the Quiz Window. You may like to play the sequence again all the way through.

Quiz Window Key:

1 1949; 2 for outdoor activities: walking, climbing, cycling, etc.; 3 1 Manchester, 2 Liverpool, 3 Sheffield; 4 It was completely changed (factories created money and employment for many people but also brought problems like pollution); 5 a mixture of smoke and fog; 6 27 million

After you watch

Discussion

Explain what students have to do and put them in groups to carry out the task. Go round the class noting mistakes to deal with later and helping out with language where necessary. When the groups have finished, get them to choose the five most important criteria from their list. Have a class feedback session and see whether all the groups agree on these five criteria.

Project

Explain what students have to do. Put them into groups to list their ideas. Go round the class noting mistakes to deal with later and helping out with language where necessary.

Either get groups to compare their ideas or have a class feedback session and pool all their ideas.

Language Window

◆ Go through the language summary with the class.

◆ Ask students to do the exercises individually or in pairs.

Key:

1 a bought; b 've cut; c played; d was; e Have you seen; f Did you see; g We haven't been; h Have you finished

2 a Have / seen; b Did / see; c did / know / was / have / been; d has stolen; e have you had; f left / got

Read and write

1 This activity asks students to identify the general meaning of each paragraph and in doing so to appreciate the structure of the letter.

Key:

c, a, b, d, e

2 Students now read the text more carefully for more detailed meaning.

Key:

a 5 houses not 15.
b The land is often used – by dog owners and as a path.
c It is very quiet.
d True.
e No – there is a shortage of housing.

3 Before students attempt this question, it might be a good idea to elicit ideas and arguments that students could use in their letter. They can write the letter in class or for homework.

7 Health

Topic content

This unit looks at different aspects of health in Britain: the National Health Service and how it works, what people have to pay for and what is free, common causes of death, private and alternative medical treatment, how people are staying healthy and life expectancy.

Teachers can find out more information on this subject in *Britain, The Country and its People: an introduction for learners of English* by James O'Driscoll, published by Oxford University Press, 1997.

Language focus

Open conditionals

Vocabulary content

energy, health care, general practitioner (GP), prescription, an operation, a specialist, treatment, heart disease, cancer, reflexology, homeopathy, acupuncture, life expectancy

Suggested procedures

◆ Use the Quiz Window to arouse students' interest and find out how much they already know about the topic area. Do not go through the answers until after the students have viewed the unit.

◆ Use the Word Window to familiarize students with some of the new vocabulary they are likely to meet. Introduce other suggested vocabulary if necessary.

◆ Work through the video and the activities sequence by sequence. You may need to play the sequences more than once so that students gain a satisfactory understanding. Use the Review activity for a final global viewing.

◆ Alternatively, you may want to play the whole unit through once straightaway. You can use the Quiz Window to focus students' attention while doing this. The follow-up viewing can then be divided into sections so that students can work through the other activities.

◆ The Language Window draws a particular grammar point from the unit, highlights it, and provides follow-up exercises and reinforcement.

◆ The After you watch and Read and write sections provide a variety of topic-linked follow-up activities.

Before you watch

These **Before you watch** activities are designed to arouse students' interest in the topic and pre-teach some of the vocabulary necessary for understanding the unit.

Quiz Window

◆ Find out what students already know about how the British health system. It might be a good starting point to get them to explain their own health system and then ask them in what way they think the British system might be different.

◆ Put students in pairs to complete the Quiz Window. Stress that they are not expected to be able to answer all the questions in the Quiz Window but that by the end of the lesson they should have all the answers. Encourage students to speculate on the answers as this will motivate them to watch the unit.

◆ The answers to the Quiz Window are given in the Review section.

Word Window

◆ Students can do these exercises on their own or in pairs. They should use dictionaries if necessary.

Key:

1

PEOPLE	PLACES	DISEASES	TREATMENT
general practitioner (GP)	hospital	cancer	ointment
	surgery	influenza	nose drops
	operating	malaria	chemotherapy
dentist	theatre	bronchitis	tablets
specialist	clinic	appendicitis	physiotherapy
chiropractor	pharmacy		surgery
nurse			

2 You get a receipt from a shop as proof that you have paid for something:
They wouldn't give me my money back because I didn't have the receipt.
Your doctor gives you a prescription for medicine:
The doctor gave me a prescription for some antibiotics and told me to come back in three weeks.
A recipe tells you how to cook something:
That soup was delicious. Can you let me have the recipe?

While you watch

To help student's comprehension of the unit, the viewing is split up into four sequences.

Sequence 1 ▢▢▢▢

(up to: … *million prescriptions a year.*)

1 Check students know what the different places are.

   ▶ Play the sequence.

   Key:

   The following places should be ticked: swimming pool, hospital, pharmacy, doctor's surgery.

2 Give students time to look through he questions.

   ▶ Play the sequence again.

   Key:

   1 c; 2 b; 3 b; 4 a; 5 b

Sequence 2 ▢▢▢▢

(up to: … *and for trips to the dentist.*)

1 Give students time to look at the pictures so that they know what they are looking for.

   ▶ Play the sequence.

   Key:

   1 ✓; 2 ✗; 3 ✓; 4 ✓; 5 ✓; 6 ✗

2 Ask students to look at the exercise and tick the appropriate boxes.

   ▶ Play the sequence again while students check and / or change their answers.

   Key:

1948		TODAY
✓	visits to the doctor	✓
✓	visits to the dentist	
✓	treatment	✓
✓	operations	✓
✓	prescriptions	
✓	eye tests	
✓	glasses	

Sequence 3 ▢▢▢▢

(up to: … *alternative medical practitioners in Britain than NHS doctors.*)

◆ Give students time to look at both questions.

   ▶ Play the sequence. If necessary, play it again so that students are able to catch all the necessary information.

Key

1 No of employees: nearly a million
   Cost: almost £40 billion a year
   Problems: people have to wait to see a specialist or for an operation

2 a Because they have to wait in the NHS
   b more than 36,000 / more than there are GPs

Sequence 4 ▢▢▢▢

(to the end)

◆ Ask students to complete the speech bubbles before they watch the sequence. In the first bubble they should complete each blank with a word. In the second with a number – they will have to make a guess at the numbers. You could make it a competition to see who gets the closest numbers.

   ▶ Play the sequence.

   Key:

   1 get; 2 stay; 3 eat; 4 meat; 5 fruit; 6 271; 7 3,000

Review

Students should go back and add to or change what they have written in the Quiz Window. You may like to play the sequence again all the way through.

Quiz Window Key:

1 c National Health Service; 2 for an operation, for tests, for treatment, to visit someone, for an X-ray, etc.
3 b cancer, a heart disease; 5 men to 74; women to 79

After you watch

Competition

Explain the activity to the class. Give them a time limit to list the differences. Five minutes is probably quite long enough. While they are making their lists, go round the class noting mistakes to deal with later. When they have finished, have a class feedback session to see which pair / group has thought of the most differences.

Project

If possible, take into class some health promotion posters to give students ideas as to what they can do. Go through the instructions for the project. Elicit suggestions and ideas both for poster designs and for the sort of language that could be used on them. Put students in pairs or small groups to design their posters.

Put the completed posters round the classroom walls. Have a vote to decide which is the best.

Language Window

◆ Go through the language summary with the class.

◆ Ask students to do the exercises either individually or in pairs.

Key:

1 1 If the weather's fine, they always have lunch in the garden.
   2 If anything moves, the alarm goes off.
   3 If you are nervous, take some deep breaths to relax yourself.
   4 If you are early, wait outside until I arrive.
   5 If you get hungry, there's some cheese in the fridge.
   6 If you want to play well, you have to practise.

2 a will be, don't (do not) see
   b arrives, 'll (will) fire
   c give, 'll (will) send
   d 'll (will) make, buy
   e 'll (will) clean, hoover
   f work, 'll (will) fail
   g walk, 's raining
   h don't (do not), 'll (will) never speak

Read and write

These activities can be done in class or for homework.

1 This activity encourages students to look for the general meaning of each paragraph and to work out how the article is structured.

   Key:

   c, e, a, d, b

2 This activity demands a more detailed reading of the text.

   Key:

   1 Breakfast should contain 25% of the day's calories.

   2 In the morning the brain needs sugar.

   3 Scrambled egg and smoked salmon is full of protein.

   4 Porridge is full of carbohydrates.

   5 Fried food is full of fat and calories.

3 Give students time to think about what they might write. They could discuss their ideas in pairs. They could write the article for homework or in class.

8 Law and order

Topic content

This unit looks at law and order in Britain: the police and what they do, crime and criminals, the court system and the prison system.

Teachers can find out more information on this subject in *Britain, The Country and its People: an introduction for learners of English* by James O'Driscoll, published by Oxford University Press, 1997.

Language focus

Present and Past simple passive

Vocabulary content

under what circumstances ... ?, to grab, a foot officer, to socialize, the fight against crime, to record, theft, to commit a crime, to arrest, court, a case, armed robbery, murder, the dock, the defendant, the judge, the jury, a sentence, guilty, proportion, to abolish

Suggested procedures

◆ Use the Quiz Window to arouse students' interest and find out how much they already know about the topic area. Do not go through the answers until after the students have viewed the unit.

◆ Use the Word Window to familiarize students with some of the new vocabulary they are likely to meet. Introduce other suggested vocabulary if necessary.

◆ Work through the video and the activities sequence by sequence. You may need to play the sequences more than once so that students gain a satisfactory understanding. Use the Review activity for a final global viewing.

◆ Alternatively, you may want to play the whole unit through once straightaway. You can use the Quiz Window to focus students' attention while doing this. The follow-up viewing can then be divided into sections so that students can work through the other activities.

◆ The Language Window draws a particular grammar point from the unit, highlights it, and provides follow-up exercises and reinforcement.

◆ The After you watch and Read and write sections provide a variety of topic-linked follow-up activities.

Before you watch

These Before you watch activities are designed to arouse students' interest in the topic and pre-teach some of the vocabulary necessary for understanding the unit.

Quiz Window

◆ Find out what students already know about law and order in Britain. What is their picture of the British police? Do they feel Britain is a law-abiding nation or not? Do they know anything about the British system of justice and punishment?

◆ Put students in pairs to complete the Quiz Window. Stress that they are not expected to be able to answer all the questions in the Quiz Window but that by the end of the lesson they should have all the answers. Encourage students to speculate on the answers as this will motivate them to watch the unit.

◆ The answers to the Quiz Window are given in the Review section.

Word Window

Students can do these exercises in pairs or individually. They should use dictionaries if necessary.

Key:

1	burglary	He broke into a house and stole something.
	murder	She killed someone.
	armed robbery	They went into a bank with guns and stole some money.
	vandalism	He smashed all the windows in a phone box.
	smuggling	He brought drugs into the country under his clothes.
	theft	She stole someone's handbag in a restaurant.
	blackmail	She threatened to send the photographs to his wife unless he paid her £1000.
	shoplifting	They stole clothes from a department store.
	kidnapping	They said they would return the child for £1 million.
	car theft	He stole a car.

2 1 a burglar; 2 a murderer; 3 an armed robber;
4 a vandal; 5 a smuggler; 6 a thief; 7 a blackmailer;
8 a shoplifter; 9 a kidnapper; 10 a car thief

While you watch

To help students' comprehension of the unit, the viewing is split up into five sequences.

Sequence 1 ☐☐☐☐

(up to: *Did they see anything?*)

1 Tell the students that will see a scene in a police station. On the first viewing all they have to do is get a general idea of what is happening and what has happened?

   Play the sequence.

   Key:

   Someone stole a bag belonging to one of the girls while they were having lunch in a park.

2 Ask students to look at the speech bubbles. A strong class might be able to fill in some of the blanks at this stage.

   Play the sequence again. If necessary pause at appropriate moments to give students time to complete the blanks.

   Key:

   Can you tell me when this happened, please?
   OK. Where were you?
   Was there anybody else there?
   Did they see anything?
   Under what circumstances was it taken?

   For the girls' answers see the transcript. Students should be expected to understand the gist of what they say rather than every word.

Sequence 2 ☐☐☐☐

(up to: ... *police officers in Britain.*)

1 Ask students to look at the exercise so that they know what to look out for when you play the sequence.

   Play the sequence.

   Key:

   The police officer talks to: a car driver, two young men, two girls

2 Emphasize that students should make notes rather than write down every word.

   Play the sequence again while students make notes.

   Key:

   7 am – 7 pm   – very beautiful
                  – nice places for tourists and locals

   7 pm – 7 am   – like Manchester and London
                  – very busy
                  – a lot of people out socialising and drinking

Sequence 3 ☐☐☐☐

(up to: ... *more men than women commit crimes.*)

1 See the introduction for what to do if your video player does not have a sound only facility.

   Play the sequence without the pictures. Allow time for students to discuss their ideas as to what the pictures might be. Have a feedback session and pool ideas.

   Play the sequence again with the pictures. Give students time to compare their ideas with what they actually saw.

2 Ask students to match the sentence halves.

   Play the sequence again if necessary.

   Key:

   In 1999 ...
   about five million crimes were recorded.
   two million of these crimes were theft.
   over a million cars were broken into or stolen.
   nearly a million burglaries were committed.

Sequence 4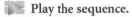

(up to: ... *what the sentence will be.*)

1 Ask students to look at the question before viewing the sequence.

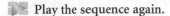 Play the sequence.

Key:

in a courtroom

2 Ask students to look at the questions. A strong class may already be able to answer some or all of them.

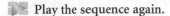 Play the sequence again.

Key:

a people who have committed less important crimes
b people who have committed more serious crimes
c the defendant
d the jury
e the judge

Sequence 5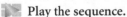

(to the end)

◆ Ask students what they imagine the inside of a prison to be like. Elicit ideas and make notes on the board. Ask students to read through the questions so they know what information they are listening for.

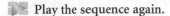 Play the sequence.

Key:

1 a over 70,000; 2 b no death penalty for murder;
3 a become a hotel

Cultural background

It is commonly believed that there is no death penalty at all in Britain. This is not actually true. The death penalty for murder was abolished in 1969 but it still theoretically remains as a punishment for treason. However, it is difficult to imagine circumstances in which a judge would feel it necessary to pass a death sentence.

Review

Students should go back and add to or change what they have written in the Quiz Window. You may like to play the sequence again all the way through.

Quiz Window Key:

1 a T; b T; c F.
2 (above) a courtroom; (below) a prison
3 1 a judge; 2 a jury
4 b

After you watch

Problem solving

1 Put students in pairs or small groups to do the vocabulary activity. Check their answers before moving on to the next exercise.

Key:

1 fine: you pay money to the court
2 community service: you carry out work to help other people
3 probation: you report to an official at regular intervals
4 prison sentence: you go to prison
5 suspended prison sentence: you will go to prison if you commit another crime within a certain period of time
6 discharge: you are allowed to go free

2 In the same pairs or groups, check that students understand what they have to do. While they discuss what punishment should be given in each situation, go round monitoring language and helping where necessary. When some groups have finished, have a feedback session and find out what the different groups felt.

Discussion

◆ First give students time to read the speech bubbles on their own and decide how they feel about each one.

◆ Then put them into pairs or small groups to discuss and compare their answers. During the discussion help students out with language where necessary and note down frequent mistakes for later remedial treatment.

Language Window

◆ Go through the language summary with the class.

◆ Ask students to do the exercises individually or in pairs.

Key:

1   1 b He was fined £500.
    2 a It's given every year to the writer of the best book on gardening.
    3 a So I took it back.
    4 b I was stopped by the police.
    5 a He invented the telephone.
2   a Where was it made?
    b She was taken to hospital last night.
    c When was he arrested?
    d It's made of paper.
    e Where is it spoken?
    f The front door is locked at six o'clock.
    g When was it built?
    h He was interviewed last week.

Read and write

1   Students should skim the five articles quickly and decide which headline goes with which article.

Key:

1   c Boy arrested over bomb in school
2   b Robbers fire at police
3   e Game ends in shooting
4   d Safe theft not safe
5   a Drug find – four held

2   Students should read the articles more carefully and choose the best endings.

Key:

1 a; 2 a; 3 a; 4 b; 5 b

3   Students can write their article in class or for homework. Whichever course of action you adopt, it would be a good idea to make sure students have some ideas and all the necessary vocabulary before they start writing.

Transcripts

Introduction

LEONIE Welcome to Window on Britain 2. In this programme we're going to look at some important areas of British life.

We're going to find out what the British do on holiday; what kinds of animals are common in Britain; what people watch and read; and what they do in their free time. We're also going to look at the environment, health, and law and order.

1 Work

LEONIE First, let's look at work in Britain. Where do British people work? How many hours do they work? And what jobs do they do?

The population of Great Britain is almost 59 million. About 27 million people work ... 15 million men and 12 million women. They can start work at the age of 16.

About 1.5 million people are unemployed. They haven't got jobs. Job Centres like this one help them to find work.

Most people work full-time. On average, men in Britain work 44 hours a week. Most men retire at the age of 65. Women work about 31 hours a week and usually retire at the age of 60. For women the average is less because many of them work part-time.

So what kinds of work do British people do? Over a million people work in the building industry.

In the past Britain was famous for manufacturing. In the nineteenth century, factories and shipyards in Scotland, Wales and the north of England produced cotton, machines and ships to make Britain the world's leading industrial nation.

Other industries developed in the twentieth century. This is the Jaguar car factory in Coventry. The first of the famous Jaguar cars appeared in 1935, and production started here in 1951. The American car company Ford bought Jaguar in 1989. Over 2,000 people work a this factory, and they produce about 200 cars a day.

Although manufacturing is still important, more and more people now work in offices and spend a lot of the day working with computers.

One very big business in Britain today is finance ... money. London's the number one financial centre in Europe and number three in the world behind New York and Tokyo.

Retailing is important, too ... selling goods to people like you and me. Eight of the top ten retail companies in Europe are British, and four of the top ten food retailers. Do you know any of these British companies?

Of course, we're now living in the twenty-first century and hi-tech industries are very important. This is Research Machines, a company near Oxford. They make computers and software.

Most British people get 20 working days holiday every year. There are also eight public holidays. We call these Bank Holidays because they were days when banks closed.

LEONIE What do you do?

SCHOOL TEACHER I'm a schoolteacher

HELICOPTER PILOT I'm a helicopter pilot.

BOOKSELLER I'm a bookseller.

SALES REP I'm a sales rep.

LECTURER I'm a lecturer.

PILOT I'm an airline pilot.

TOUR GUIDE I'm an Oxford Walking Tour guide.

LEONIE How many hours do you work a week?

SALES REP Sixty, eighty, it depends.

SCHOOL TEACHER During school term about sixty.

HELICOPTER PILOT I guess about thirty to forty.

BOOKSELLER I think it's thirty-seven and a half.

PILOT I actually fly for about twenty hours, but probably work for about fifty.

LECTURER Round about twelve contact hours of teaching.

TOUR GUIDE Anything from three days a week to seven days a week.

LEONIE What do you like about your job?

PILOT It's fun.

BOOKSELLER I love serving customers.

SALES REP Freedom. It's up to me to arrange it the way I like.

LECTURER Oh, meeting young people.

LEONIE What do you like about your job?

TOUR GUIDE I meet people from all round the world.

SCHOOL TEACHER The long holidays.

HELICOPTER PILOT I get home every night, and I don't have to think about anything else.

LEONIE What don't you like about it?

HELICOPTER PILOT Getting up at five o'clock in the morning.

LECTURER Administration, a lot of paperwork.

PILOT I don't like folding lots of shirts to go away on trips.

SCHOOL TEACHER Working at weekends.

TOUR GUIDE What don't I like? Rain!

LEONIE These days we can send information all over the world at the touch of a button. As more people go on-line, so more people are working from home. Well over half a million people work mainly from home. It's easy, it's convenient, and you can have a cup of tea when you want one.

2 Holidays

LEONIE When do British people go on holiday? How much time do they take? And where do they go?

Like millions of other British people, I go on holiday in the summer. Although July and August are the most popular months, not everyone takes their holidays at the same time. Lots of people take a two-week break, but they can choose when to take it.

Going abroad for a holiday is now very popular. British people make almost 40 million holiday trips every year. That's seven times more than in 1970. Florida and the Caribbean are popular with some holidaymakers, but 85% of foreign holidays are in Western Europe. Spain is the number one choice for many people. Over 25% of all British holidaymakers go there.

Why do so many British people go abroad for their holidays? Because of the British weather. Sometimes there isn't very much sun!

But not everyone goes abroad. The traditional British seaside holiday is still very popular.

In the nineteenth century, there weren't any cars or planes. People travelled by train from the big cities to seaside towns such as Blackpool, Bournemouth ... and here, Brighton, which is only 100 kilometres from London.

People come here to swim, windsurf, sunbathe or just sit in a deckchair. Brighton is a place for family holidays because there are lots of things to do. They all have a good time ... and it doesn't matter how old you are!

People stay in hotels, guest houses and bed and breakfasts.

Some people camp in tents or stay in caravans. This is a cheaper type of holiday.

Everyone hopes for a lot of sunshine and not too much rain!

Over 2 million British people spend their holiday in Devon or Cornwall in the south-west of England. In the north, the Lake District and Scotland are both very popular.

Surprisingly, London isn't popular. Very few British people go there. How many? Only about a quarter of a million.

Not everyone wants to spend 2 weeks lying on a beach. Many British people have activity holidays, doing things such as climbing, cycling, walking in the hills, or …

… sailing on a narrow boat along a canal. You can travel gently through the countryside and spend a little time visiting interesting places. You don't have to book a hotel, because you sleep on the boat. It's very different to everyday life, and very relaxing!

3 Animals

LEONIE Animals are very important to the British ... at home, in the wild, and on the farm. What are the most popular pets in Britain? What wild animals are there? What are the most common farm animals? Well, there are more than 11 millions cows. We use them for milk and for beef.

There are also a lot of pigs ... 7 million, in fact.

But there are even more sheep than pigs and cows together. There are about 44 and a half million sheep in Britain.

There are lots of birds on farms, too, such as, turkeys, ducks ... and chickens. Altogether there are an amazing 172 million farm birds.

There are about 30,000 different kinds of animals in Britain. The fallow deer is one of the most attractive wild animals. It's also one of the easiest to see because they live all over Britain. Fallow deer live in the countryside but you can see them in some parks too.

One of the smallest wild animals is the field mouse.

The largest wild animal is the red deer. Many years ago they lived all over the countryside, but now red deer live mainly in the Scottish Highlands.

The badger, of course, is much smaller. You can easily recognise a badger because of its black and white nose. They usually come out at night so you'll be lucky to see one.

Rabbits are easier to see, especially early in the morning and in the evening.

This is a hedgehog, the only British animal with spines.

Foxes usually live in the countryside. As more and more countryside is disappearing, some foxes are learning how to live in towns.

However, not all animals are so good at changing their habits, and some animals need protection from others. This is a red squirrel. Two hundred years ago red squirrels lived all over Britain. Then in the 19th century the grey squirrel came to Britain from North America. The grey squirrel is a little bit bigger than the red squirrel and it's much better at finding food.

Nowadays you can only find red squirrels in Scotland and some parts of England.

The golden eagle also needs protection ... but from humans. It's one the rarest British animals. There are just over 800 golden eagles left in the wild. They are one of the largest British birds and one of the most beautiful. There are a total of 116 protected species of animal in Britain.

Horses are very important in Britain. We ride them in sports such as racing and polo, or just for fun. The police also use horses to control crowds. This is Fred. Isn't he beautiful?

Because they like animals, the British give money to two societies in particular. One is the RSPCA, the Royal Society for the Prevention of Cruelty to Animals. It started in 1824 and was the first society in the world to protect animals.

The other is the RSPB, the Royal Society for the Protection of Birds. This started in 1889.

And, of course, a lot of British people have pets. In fact, over 50% of British homes have a pet. Cats, dogs and fish are the most popular. There are 8 million cats in Britain, nearly 7 million dogs and 28 million fish. It's amazing, isn't it?

LEONIE Have you got a pet?

ESME I've got one dog

LEONIE What's its name?

ESME It's called Henry.

LUCY I've got one cat called Katy.

TOM I have one kitten called Rasputin.

ALEX I've got a pet tortoise. His name's Harry.

AARON I've got a goldfish called Oxo.

PETER Yes I have a pet and his name's Barney. He's a rabbit.

LEONIE When your pet gets ill, you'll have to come here ... to the vet's. Vets are doctors for animals. They usually look after farm animals and pets.

This is the Beaumont Veterinary Hospital in Oxford. Five full-time and two part-time vets work here. The majority of the animals that they treat here are dogs, cats and rabbits.

VET ... her knee here and that's what I can feel ... and that's what the vet who saw her yesterday said. We've got two choices in terms of what to do with her: one is to have her in for an x-ray tomorrow, the other is to keep her on medication for a while, on pain killers, and see if ...

LEONIE The British really love their animals. Walk on, Fred.

4 Media

LEONIE Hi. We're going to look at the media in Britain. We're going to find out about television, radio and the Internet. But first, what do you know about British newspapers and magazines?

The British love their newspapers. Two out of three British people over the age of 15 read a newspaper every day. That's about 26 million people. Even more people read a paper on Sundays. What do they read?

The two most popular daily newspapers are tabloids ... the Sun and the Mirror. Over three and half million people buy the Sun every day and over two and a quarter million buy the Mirror. In tabloid papers you'll find more gossip, more human interest stories, more pictures ... and not very much serious news.

These newspapers are larger. They're called broadsheets or quality papers. About a million people buy the Daily Telegraph and about 700,000 buy The Times. There's also The Independent and The Guardian. In these papers you'll find more news, more serious articles and fewer pictures.

Altogether there are about 130 daily and Sunday papers in Britain ... some national, some local. There are also over 6,500 different magazines!

Of course, nowadays not everyone actually buys a newspaper. Some people read their newspaper online. Over 75,000 people visit this website every day. The number of people in Britain who use the Internet is increasing all the time.

A lot of people also listen to the news on the radio.

NEWSREADER BBC Radio 4. The news at seven o'clock. The Chancellor, Gordon Brown ...

LEONIE The BBC is the British Broadcasting Corporation. It has five national radio stations, 39 local stations, and two terrestrial television channels.

The BBC is not commercial ... there's no advertising during their programmes. British people have to buy a television licence every year. The BBC uses the money from this to make television and radio programmes. Here they're filming *Middlemarch*, the classic novel by George Eliot.

There are three other terrestrial TV channels. There's ITV, that's Independent Television, Channel 4, and Channel 5. These are all commercial and have advertising. Of course, there's satellite and cable TV, too. There are lots of satellite and cable channels.

On average British people watch almost 24 hours of television a week. Most households have at least one television and 46% of British children have a television in their bedroom.

LEONIE How often do you watch TV?

AARON Nearly every day.

CALLY Quite a lot, every night.

MARAL Usually, I watch television every night.

NABILA I watch it for about two hours a day. Not very much.

ESME Each day I watch an hour of television.

LEONIE What's your favourite programme?

NABILA My favourite programme is *Neighbours*.

ESME My favourite programme is *The Simpsons*.

PETER I like sport, mainly, on television: football, rugby.

MARAL My favourite programmes are the soap operas like *East Enders*.

JAMES My favourite programmes are *East Enders*, *The Simpsons* and *Friends*.

TOM My favourite programmes MTV.

LUCY My favourite programmes are *Friends* and *The Simpsons*.

LEONIE What are you going to watch tonight?

NABILA Tonight I'm going to watch *Neighbours* and *Friends*.

ESME Tonight I'll probably watch *Top of the Pops*.

LUCY I'm going to watch *Neighbours* and *Friends*.

MARAL Tonight I'll probably watch *Top of the Pops* and *Friends*.

LEONIE Eighty-four percent of British homes have a video recorder – that's more than in any other European country.

LEONIE What kind of videos do you watch?

NABILA I watch action and sci-fi videos

ESME I like comedy films.

CALLY I like old films like *Casablanca* and *Citizen Kane*.

TOM I watch skateboarding and rollerblading videos.

LUCY I would normally watch comedy videos.

LEONIE It's interesting that in Britain more people have a television than a washing machine. But my washing machine has a terrible picture!

5 Leisure

LEONIE British people spend their free time in a lot of different ways. They do sport, they watch sport, they visit interesting places, and they have hobbies. Have you tried any of these?

LEONIE What do you do in your free time?

NABILA I like to watch television and listen to music a lot. But I do go on the Internet as well.

TOM I like to skateboard and rollerblade in my free time.

PETER I play rugby in my free time for Oxford Rugby Club. And I also play tennis.

MARAL In my free time I usually play sport, which is usually tennis if the weather is nice or swimming.

JAMES I like playing rugby. I'm a member of a rugby team. I like swimming, playing tennis and football.

AARON I play football for a football team. I play a lot of tennis as well.

CALLY I play rugby or cricket, or go sailing.

ESME I play sport, go into town, see my friends.

LUCY In my free time I go to a drama group and a dance group.

LEONIE So what are the top ten leisure activities in Britain?

The most popular activity for British people outside their own home is ... going to the pub. Over the last ten or twenty years pubs have changed a lot. People don't just go to the pub for a drink. Almost all pubs serve meals nowadays and many pubs have live music, karaoke competitions and quiz nights.

The second most popular activity is going to a restaurant. And the third?

Young people, especially, like going out for fast food. The number of fast food restaurants in Britain has increased about 10 times since 1982. And after fast food?

The fourth most popular activity is ... going to the library. Surprisingly, this is more popular than going to the cinema ...

... although the number of people going to the cinema has almost doubled since 1980, and the number of cinemas has more than doubled, too.

Many people visit historic buildings. This is Kingston Lacey, a beautiful seventeenth century house with lovely gardens.

Nearby is Corfe Castle. It is over one thousand years old and full of history.

Short break holidays both abroad and in Britain are very popular.

A lot of young people go to discos and nightclubs.

And, of course, watching sport is a big free time activity.

Favourite sports include football ... horseracing ... and cricket, a traditional English sport.

Art galleries and museums are popular, too. This is the Ashmolean Museum in Oxford. The Ashmolean is the oldest museum in Britain and has been part of the University of Oxford since 1683. They have a wonderful collection here including these beautiful sculptures. 200,000 people visit this museum every year. Like many museums in Britain, admission is free.

What other places do people like to visit?

Almost 3 million people visit Alton Towers every year. This ride is called Nemesis. And this one is called Oblivion.

Then there's Madame Tussaud's ... the Tower of London ... Legoland ... and the London Eye. The London Eye opened in March 2000 and is one of London's most popular attractions.

But what do the British do at home in their free time? Well, listening to the radio or to CDs is popular. So is reading. And people spend a lot of time visiting or entertaining their friends and family. But the most popular activity? You've guessed it. It's watching TV.

6 Environment

LEONIE This is the Peak District National Park. It covers an area of about one thousand five hundred square kilometres in the centre of England. The government created National Parks in 1949 to protect the environment.

Britain is a small country with a large population. Nearly fifty-nine million people live here, seventy-five percent in towns and cities. The Peak District lies between Manchester and Sheffield and near several other large towns and cities. A third of the population of Britain can get here in less than an hour. In fact there are over 22 million visitors every year.

On the River Mersey near Liverpool, not far from the Peak District, we see what industry can do to the environment.

Here in the Midlands and the north of England the Industrial Revolution changed the face of the British countryside. Factories create money and employment but they also bring problems.

Pollution has been a problem in Britain since the nineteenth century. At that time London became famous for its smog ... a mixture of smoke and fog. Smog continued to be a big problem in the twentieth century, too. In 1952, four thousand people died when the smog lasted for several days. Since then the government has introduced laws to control pollution. For example, people aren't allowed to burn coal in towns and cities.

But new threats to the environment have appeared.

There are now twenty-seven million cars, vans and lorries on the roads in Britain. A quarter of families have two or more cars. On average, the British use buses and trains for only one out of ten journeys.

Many cities have taken action to deal with increasing traffic. This is the High Street in Oxford. Only buses, taxis and bicycles can use this street during the day. Many other British cities now have traffic-free areas.

Looking after the environment has become an important part of British life. In such a crowded country it's essential to protect the countryside so that people can enjoy it.

LEONIE Why do you come to the Peak District?

GIRL Well there's lovely areas around here and there's loads of walks. There's nature walks all the way round as you can see. And it's just a nice area for families to come.

WOMAN 1 It's absolutely beautiful. I love walking here, and there are certain parts I come to quite often.

MAN 1 You get a lot of variation. There's valleys, there's water, streams, rivers, lakes.

MAN 2 Fresh air, you have a good appetite when you've been here.

WOMAN 2 I love the countryside so I love to come for a walk. And I like to look at the wildlife.

WOMAN 3 There are such lovely places to see and nice walks to do, and the people are very friendly. There's just so much to do in the area. It's a very nice area.

LEONIE And when the weather's good, it's really beautiful, isn't it?

7 Health

LEONIE In Britain today people are putting time, money, and energy into keeping well and keeping fit. Health care's important. So is diet. And so is fitness!

If you're ill in Britain, you go to see your GP. A GP is a general practitioner, or family doctor.

There are over 36,000 GPs in Britain and about a third of them are women. Each GP has nearly 2,000 patients. If you need medicine, your GP will write a prescription for you to take to a chemist's or pharmacy.

You don't have to pay to see your doctor, but you will probably have to pay part of the cost of your medicine, unless you belong to one of the groups of people who get their medicine free, for example, you're a student, or over 60, or expecting a baby.

Chemists prepare about 505 million prescriptions a year.

If you need to see a specialist doctor, or have medical tests or an operation, your doctor will send you to a hospital like this.

This is the John Radcliffe Hospital in Oxford. In Britain most doctors and hospitals are part of the NHS, the National Health Service.

All NHS hospital treatment and operations are free. In fact, the NHS provides free medical care for everyone in Britain from the very young … to the very old.

When the NHS started in 1948, it provided free visits to doctors and dentists; free treatment, free prescriptions, free eye tests and free glasses. But today many people have to pay for prescriptions, for eye tests and glasses, and for trips to the dentist.

Britain has one of the highest levels of heart disease in the western world. It also has a very high level of cancer.

Nearly a million people work in the National Health Service in Britain, and it costs almost £40 billion a year. It's a lot of money … and there are still problems. People sometimes have to wait a long time before they can see a specialist or have an operation.

Because of this, many people see private doctors and use other kinds of treatment, or alternative medicine, like reflexology, homeopathy, and acupuncture. It really doesn't hurt at all. In fact, there are more alternative medical practitioners in Britain than NHS doctors.

Medicine helps people get better, diet helps them stay healthy. If you eat well, you'll probably have a longer and healthier life. Nowadays British people eat less red meat and more fresh fruit and vegetables than in the past.

New medicines and better diet have raised life expectancy. On average British men live to the age of 74, British women to 79. Many people live longer than that. In 1952, only 271 people reached the age of 100. Nowadays the total's about 3,000 a year. I hope to see you on my hundredth birthday!

FIRST POLICE OFFICER Can you tell me when this happened, please?

FIRST STUDENT It was about half an hour ago, at one o'clock.

FIRST POLICE OFFICER OK, and where were you, and under what circumstances was it taken?

SECOND STUDENT We were in the park, and we were eating our lunch. And then a man suddenly arrived and he stole my bag. He was a tall man with fair hair. And he grabbed my bag, and then he ran away.

FIRST POLICE OFFICER What I need to do is complete a report.

LEONIE One important part of the work of the British police is to help the local community.

FIRST POLICE OFFICER OK. Was there anybody else there? Did they see anything?

LEONIE Police officers are often seen on the streets of British towns and cities. Unlike police in many other countries, these officers don't carry guns.

SECOND POLICE OFFICER I've covered the city for a good ten years as a foot officer. I've found that a pleasure to do that, and the locals have been very supportive. I think the public's view of the police, and the police's view of the public is very very similar. And we work very hard with the community to try and solve their problems. I would say Oxford during the day, 7 a.m. to 7 p.m., is like every city very beautiful, it's got a lot of nice places where the tourists and the locals can go. And then at night time, 7 o'clock onwards, it's like Manchester or London. It becomes very busy, a lot of people out, socialising, drinking; and the drink then adds to your problems.

LEONIE There are about one hundred and fifty thousand police officers in Britain. Another important part of their work is the fight against crime. In 1999, about five million crimes were recorded.

Two million of these crimes were theft. Half of these involved cars. Over a million cars were broken into or stolen. And nearly a million burglaries were committed. In Britain, five times more men than women commit crimes.

After people are arrested, they come to somewhere like this ... a court. In Scotland the system is a little different, but in England and Wales there are two main types of court: the Magistrates' Court and the Crown Court. Less important crimes are dealt with in Magistrates' Courts. These make up 95% of all criminal cases. The Crown Court deals with more important crimes, for example armed robbery or murder.

This part of the court is called the dock. The defendant sits here. And the judge sits here. Twelve ordinary people decide if the defendant is guilty or not guilty. These twelve people are called the jury. The judge decides what the sentence will be.

In the year 2000, the prison population in Britain was over 70,000. That's the second highest proportion of the population in any country in western Europe. In Britain the death penalty for murder was abolished in 1969. However, if necessary, a judge can send someone to prison for the rest of their life.

This prison was closed two years ago. Now it's going to become a hotel! But I don't think I'll stay here.

NOTES